# COMMUNICATIONS

**MICHAEL JAY**

Wayland

# CONTENTS

**First published in 1995 by**
Wayland (Publishers) Limited
61 Western Road, Hove, East
Sussex BN3 1JD, England
© Copyright 1995 Wayland
(Publishers) Limited

British Library Cataloguing in
Publication Data.
Jay, Michael
Communications. – (Science
Discovery Series)
I. Title II. Series
384.09

ISBN 0-7502-1238-1

**Acknowledgements**
*Concept* David Jefferis
*Text editor and picture research*
Michael Brown
*Illustrations* Peter Bull, Robert
Burns and James Robins

**Picture credits**
*Apple Computers* 46
*Boeing Aerospace* 24
*Bridgeman Art Library* 6(T)
*British Telecom* cover(TR), 4
*Peter Brown* 6(BL)
*Delta Archive* cover(TR), 5, 8,
9(R), 10, 12(T), 13, 14, 15, 18,
19, 22, 23, 27, 28, 29(R), 32, 33,
34, 42, 47
*Hulton-Deutsch Collection* 26
*Mat Irvine* 40
*Mary Evans Picture Library* 16
and cover(BR)
*National Maritime Museum*
12(BL)
*Philips* cover(TL)
*Redferns/Suzi Gibbons* 19(T)
*Science Photo Library* 9(T), 20
and back cover, 25(TL,TR), 30,
31, 34(TL), 35, 36, 37, 39, 41, 44
*Sharp Electronics* 29(BL)
*Sony Corporation* cover(BL), 27
*Southernprint Ltd* 11
*The British Museum* 7

*The Science Museum* 16, 21

Printed and bound in Italy by
G. Canale & C.S.p.A., Turin

# INTRODUCTION

Communications are something we use every day – we speak to people, write down messages, use the telephone, watch television. But it is easy to take these things for granted, without thinking about how they developed. And these developments are what this book is all about.

There have been three major improvements in ways of communicating – the development of the written word, the invention of the printing press, the electronic machines that have created the telecommunications world of today. And easy communications have created an explosion of knowledge, so much so that we now live in a new age, the Information Age.

We finish off the book with a look at these and other developments and the changes they may bring to our lives in the future.

▶ Earth stations like this are used to send and receive radio signals to and from communications satellites high in orbit above the Earth.

# ☀ COMMUNICATING IDEAS

Communications means the exchange of ideas and information between living things. In the animal kingdom a cat fluffs up its fur and hisses to frighten an enemy. A gorilla may beat its breast to declare dominance over a rival. A male moth may find a mate by detecting a chemical released by a female moth many kilometres away.

We humans first developed languages as a way of expressing ourselves, then created ways of recording the meanings permanently as the written word. These twin 'inventions' have enabled us to communicate complex ideas and information to each other. Just as importantly, the written word means that ideas need not be forgotten.

Technical advances over the last 400 years or so have produced reliable television and telephone links over long distances, letting people and machines exchange information at the speed of light – 300,000 kilometres per second – across the world and even out into space. Newspapers, magazines, books, TV, cinema and now computer networks allow information to be communicated world-wide in a matter of moments.

▶ A tiny selection of the thousands of newspapers and magazines currently published around the world.

# ANCIENT ALPHABETS

Piecing together the story of the written word is a job for archaeologists, researchers of old civilizations. There are huge gaps in our knowledge of how the earliest written languages developed – they were forgotten long before anyone began to take an interest in ancient history. Much of our present knowledge is based on work started by the researchers of the nineteenth century, and some discoveries have been made by sheer chance.

▲ The prehistoric cave painters of Lascaux showed many animals, including these bison.

The 20,000-year-old paintings on the walls of a cave at Lascaux in southern France are not writing as such, but they were certainly communications – colourful paintings, hunting scenes that showed stags, horses, bison and other animals. The cave was discovered by accident in September, 1940, by a group of schoolchildren out on a rabbit hunt with their dog. The dog fell down a hole, and when one of the boys clambered in to the rescue, he found himself surrounded by the strange, prehistoric paintings.

◄ Ancient Egyptian carvings on temple pillars. The Egyptians were among the first people to develop sophisticated writing.

Finding out what early writings actually mean is a task that is just like cracking a secret code. Sometimes, lettering looks like something that is already understood, other times, inspired guesswork has to be used. The Rosetta stone is one of the most famous of these. It was discovered by chance by a French soldier in 1799, during the 1798-1801 Napoleonic invasion of Egypt. Chiselled into the slab of stone – named after the place where it was found – were three sets of mysterious scripts, one a type of Greek, the others ancient Egyptian picture lettering, known as hieroglyphics. Experts back in France thought the scripts were translations of the same words, but the trouble was, no one understood a thing.

An eighteen-year-old French scholar called Jean-François Champollion (1790-1832) thought he had a clue, as some of the shapes in the Rosetta stone's inscriptions looked like Coptic, one of the languages he had already learned as a keen researcher on ancient Egypt. He had advice and help from many sources, but it was his knowledge of Coptic that enabled him – after fourteen years' effort – to decode the writing on the 2,000-year-old stone and discover the hidden meaning. It was a message from the Egyptian priesthood, honouring Ptolemy V, the king who ruled them in 196 BC. Champollion's work was remarkable because the shapes of the ancient inscriptions were nothing like the alphabetical letters we use today. This is the Roman alphabet, itself developed from earlier Greek and Phoenician writings.

## ☀ A BLIND ALPHABET

The credit for raised writing that blind people could read with their fingers belongs to Frenchman Valentine Haüy (1745-1822). According the one story, Haüy got the idea from seeing how a blind person could tell different piano keys by touch; another story says that a too-heavily printed business card gave him a clue. Either way, Haüy decided on a type style and size, and the first book with raised lettering was printed in 1784. The system that is now used was invented by another Frenchman, Louis Braille (1809-1852), in 1829. Braille used a system of raised dots, rather like the patterns on dominoes. In 1854, Braille was adopted as the official French blind reading system. In 1932, Standard English Braille was adopted for world-wide use.

# MAKING PAPER

▲ Papers come in every colour, shade and thickness. Here are just a few of the papers you can get in a good stationery shop.

Having a written alphabet was a major achievement, but chiselling out shapes into a block of stone or clay was not the best way of recording a mark. Papyrus was a major improvement: its light weight meant that it could be stored and transported easily. Papyrus was an Egyptian invention, which we think was first used some 5,000 years ago. Strips of pith were removed from the middle of tall reed-like papyrus plants that grew along the banks of the River Nile. The Egyptians laid the pith strips side by side, then covered them with a second layer, glued crosswise on top. The resulting sheet could then be carefully pressed, dried and polished, ready for use.

It was the Chinese who came up with the material we still use today – paper. No one knows the exact story, but tradition names Ts'ai Lun, who was a court official to the Chinese emperor, as the person who first made paper, in 105 AD. Among his ingredients were bits of tree bark, old rags and fish nets. Ts'ai Lun is thought to have got his idea from watching a type of wasp that made a thin-shelled nest from tiny flecks of wood fibre, chewing them to make them workable. Ts'ai Lun's paper turned out to be a winner, outperforming silk cloth as a writing surface.

Once paper-making became common in China, the technique spread to other parts of the world. Arabs learnt the secret in the eighth century from prisoners they had taken during raiding trips. Paper-making spread slowly into Europe, though for centuries it was made only by hand. The process was much the same that the ancient Chinese had used. A wood frame with a wire mesh was dipped into a porridge-like mixture of tiny wood chips and water. The mesh was lifted out, and when the water drained away, a thin layer of wood fibres remained. This was turned out and left to dry; the end result was a sheet of paper. Wood has proved to be the best material for general use, though many other things can be used, including cotton, grass, linen and even rice, which you can eat, too.

▲ **Rolls of recycled newsprint being dried before reuse. This paper plant processes about 300,000 tonnes of waste paper a year, mainly for newspapers and telephone directories.**

**The recycled paper industry is an important one – it has been estimated that just one Sunday edition of the New York Times creates some 3,600 tonnes of waste paper.**

The first machine for making paper in a continuous roll was perfected in France by Louis Robert, in 1799. Robert invented a machine that used a continuous flow of raw wood pulp, pumped onto a moving wire mesh belt. The pulp was then squeezed and heated between rollers to remove the water and dry the sheet. After this, it could then be rolled up into a big reel. He took the idea to England, where it was improved and patented by Henry and Sealy Fourdrinier. Today's paper making machines, though more refined, work in a similar way.

By combining dyes and pigments, and varying strength and weight, the world's paper manufacturers can offer an almost infinite variety of paper types, from the finest bleached-white notepaper to tough brown wrapping paper.

 ## PENS AND PENCILS

Reed pens were used by the ancient Egyptians, Greeks and Romans for writing on papyrus and parchment. They also discovered that they could make marks on wax and clay tablets using a pointed rod. This was called a stylus and was often made of bronze or bone. The Romans also used pens, made of bronze, some with nibs similar to those of today. Quill pens, usually of swan or goose feathers, were used in Europe from about 600 AD, and were popular up to the nineteenth century, when they began to be replaced by the newly invented fountain pen.

The first fountain pens were made as early as 1809, but these early models had difficulties with a free-flowing ink supply. It was not until 1884 that a successful fountain pen was made, by an American insurance salesman, Lewis Edson Waterman. It had an ink reservoir in the case, which was filled up with a dropper. Later designs had a rubber bag which could be refilled by suction direct from an ink pot. In 1952, there was even the Schnorkel, which came equipped with an extending tube that dipped into the ink!

The pencil dates from 1565, when German scientist Konrad Gesner came up with the idea of putting a graphite rod in a wooden tube. The pencil was the first real alternative to the quill pen.

A ballpoint pen was first thought up by American John J Loud in 1888, but it was rather crude and was up against the fountain pen, which was then new and highly successful. The ballpoint we know today was a 1938 invention from two Hungarians, Ladislao and Georg Biro, who aimed to make a pen that would work cleanly at high altitudes, in the British Royal Air Force's new planes. Success lay in the Biros' secret-formula thick ink, which dried almost instantly on contact with paper.

# THE PRINTING PRESS

▲ **An early printing press. Moving the big lever controlled the amount of pressure on the paper. Adjusting it correctly was part of a printer's craft, to achieve the best finished result.**

 ## A BIG BUSINESS

Printing is a huge industry today, with speed of production being a major requirement. Early mechanical presses gave a speed of about 1,100 sheets an hour. The rotary press, patented by Richard Hoe in 1844, speeded things up to 8,000 sheets, and by 1865 papers were being printed using continuous reels of paper, which was cut after printing. Using this system, 12,000 complete newspapers per hour was possible.

A key development in the story of communications was the printing press. Until then, making copies of anything was a slow business, done one at a time, by hand.

The Chinese developed the first printing methods in about the sixth century AD, but it was not for another five hundred years that the idea of movable type was put into practice, again by the Chinese. Here, individual characters were carved into hard wood. They could be arranged as required, then rearranged afterwards for use time and time again.

But the credit for the start of printing in Europe goes to the fifteenth-century German, Johannes Gutenberg. He reinvented the Chinese idea of movable type and in 1454 printed two huge volumes of the bible for the city of Mainz in Germany. He used cast metal for the movable letters, which was a huge improvement over wood, allowing sharp reproduction and much longer life before wearing out.

The print revolution, and the knowledge explosion it fuelled, spread rapidly across Europe. By 1476, wool merchant William Caxton had set up the first printing press in Britain, bringing the machine across the North Sea from Bruges in Belgium, where he had lived for several years. For the first time ever, using Gutenberg's invention, books, leaflets and soon the first newspapers, could be produced quickly, cheaply and in large numbers, allowing knowledge to be spread widely.

▲ A modern full-colour printing machine, capable of printing thousands of large sheets an hour. They are bound into book form by a binder. Machine-printing was not invented until the early nineteenth century, and the first newspaper to be printed this way was *The Times* of London, in 1814. Newspaper printing remained almost entirely black-and-white, right up until the 1980s – even today, newspapers generally use colour quite sparingly.

▼ A colour printing press builds up a picture a stage at a time, by using four coloured inks: cyan (blue), magenta (red), yellow and black. Overlaying these, one after another, creates a colour image. The full-colour effect is achieved by printing thousands of tiny dots. If you look at a printed picture – such as one on a page of this book – through a magnifying glass, you can see how the dots are arranged.

# SENDING MESSAGES

Printing and publishing do not answer every communication requirement – speed is often the most important factor. Before today's instant electronic links, the need for speed inspired many inventions and developments.

For short distances, signal flags were a good option, and were particularly useful at sea. During naval battles, secret codes were necessary for messages and battle orders, to avoid the enemy knowing what was going on. Otherwise, simple semaphore could be used, the changing positions of a pair of flags representing letters of the alphabet.

Over longer distances many systems have been used, from the smoke signals of native American Indians to message-carrying homing pigeons. Horseback relay systems were used by the Mongols of Asia and later by the Pony Express riders of nineteenth-century America. But the first real technological breakthrough was by an enterprising French engineer, Claude Chappe.

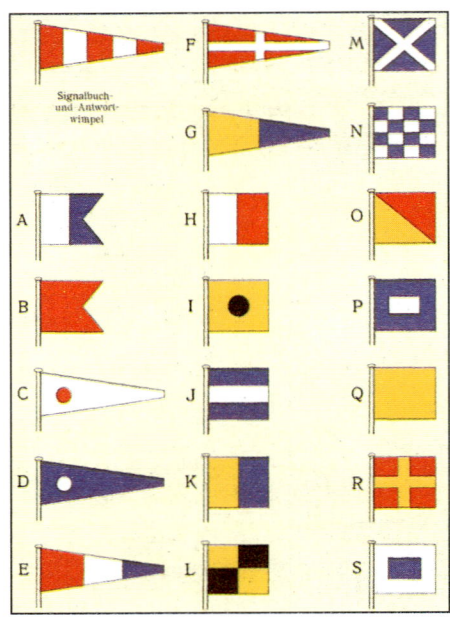

▲ This page from an old German naval manual shows a range of signal flags, each representing a letter of the alphabet.

◄ Naval signal flags were used in battles between France and Britain in the Napoleonic Wars. Here, coded orders and messages fly from the rigging.

Chappe used the optical power of the telescope as an essential part of his scheme for a communications system for the French army in the 1790s. His team built a large number of towers, each one just in sight of the other. Depending on the landscape, this could be up to about 20 km or so. Movable wooden arms were mounted on top of each tower, the arms changing position in a code system that represented letters of the alphabet. The message was passed on, relay-style, by a lookout in the next tower peering through his telescope, reading the positions of the arms. This second tower's arms were adjusted accordingly and read in turn by the lookout in the third tower in the chain, and so on.

Chappe's optical semaphore had many drawbacks – it was expensive to run, as all the towers had to be permanently manned, and bad weather was a problem. But when skies were clear, messages could be sent and received faster than ever before – the record time for one short message on Chappe's system was just three minutes over a distance of some 800 km.

▲ One of Claude Chappe's semaphore towers. The first message was sent a distance of some 230 km, between Lille and Paris, on 15 August, 1794. By the time Chappe died in 1805, his system covered much of France, with a 5,000 km network of 556 stations. It was in regular use for another 50 years.

# THE TELEGRAPH

Useful as Chappe's system was, there was strong competition from people with machines that used electricity, then still a new and rather mysterious force. Researchers found that electricity travelled very quickly along metal wires, so the idea of using it for sending messages was a good one. Not all suggestions were very practical however – Francisco Salva from Spain thought up a scheme that involved operators sending and receiving coded electric shocks! A better solution was one devised by Georges Lesage, who in 1774 built a machine that flashed messages between rooms in his residence in Geneva, Switzerland. It was too complex though, as each letter of the alphabet had to have its own separate wire.

Various schemes were devised in the early years of the nineteenth century, and the inventor of the first practical electric telegraph was a German, Baron Schilling. His equipment impressed the Russian emperor Nicholas I enough that a Schilling telegraph was built in 1832 to connect the government offices in St Petersburg with the imperial palace some distance away, at Peterhof.

▲ Samuel Morse devised a dot-dash code system with his assistant, Alfred Vail. Morse also perfected an electrical relay for the telegraph itself, an idea based on earlier talks with a fellow American, Joseph Henry. The relay behaved as a signal booster, enabling signals to travel long distances without needing massive power plants.

▼ Lesage's equipment could send messages short distances. Its complexity let it down.

Meanwhile in Britain, physicists William Cooke and Charles Wheatstone also worked on the electric telegraph and in 1837 demonstrated their equipment to the directors of a railway company. At that time the railways were the fastest means of travel, and the speedy telegraph was reckoned a good way to improve safety, by showing if there were holdups or accidents further along the line. In 1839, a 22-km telegraph line went into action, with much success.

The early telegraphs were usually laid next to railways and roads. At first, they stopped at borders between countries, so that messages had to be jotted down, then sent on again. This caused so many delays that in 1852, it was agreed that international lines could be built. Apart from safety instructions for railway companies and individuals sending messages, the booming newspaper industry became a major user of the telegraph. Headline stories which once might have taken days or weeks to arrive from distant countries, now arrived in hours or minutes. Baron Paul Julius von Reuter was among the first to use the telegraphs for news gathering, and the agency he created in 1851 is still in the news business.

▲ By the mid nineteenth century, telegraphy was a booming business. Here, dozens of operators work in the central Paris telegraph office.

In North America, the telegraph lines marched side by side with the railways, from east to west, across the continent driving the short-lived Pony Express company out of business in 1862. In 1860, this horseback relay service had been the quickest way of sending messages the 4,000-km distance between New York and San Francisco. Samuel Morse's code system became the standard way of sending messages on the American telegraphs. It was a brilliantly simple idea that used combinations of dots and dashes to represent letters and numbers. It was fairly easy to learn and quick to use, and eventually Morse code became the world standard.

▶ Cooke and Wheatstone's telegraphs used magnetic needles which swung into various positions as current passed down the telegraph wire. The wire ran by the side of the railway; the telegraph machines were in the stations.

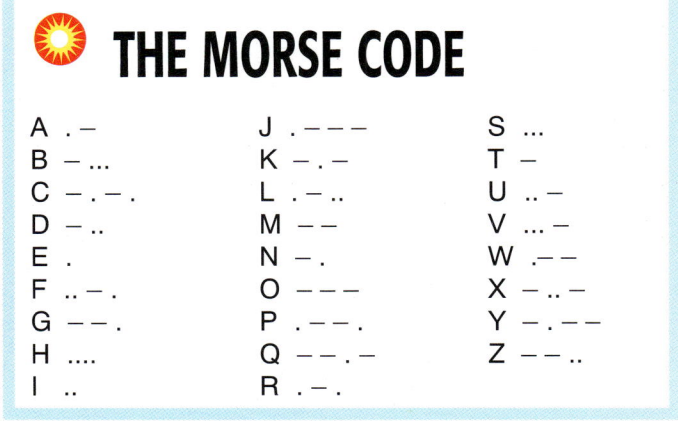

## ☀ THE MORSE CODE

| | | |
|---|---|---|
| A . — | J . — — — | S . . . |
| B — . . . | K — . — | T — |
| C — . — . | L . — . . | U . . — |
| D — . . | M — — | V . . . — |
| E . | N — . | W . — — |
| F . . — . | O — — — | X — . . — |
| G — — . | P . — — . | Y — . — — |
| H . . . . | Q — — . — | Z — — . . |
| I . . | R . — . | |

15

# THE TELEPHONE

The idea of being able to speak over a distance dates back to 1667, when Englishman Robert Hooke suggested joining two cans with a length of taut string. It is an idea that makes a good toy, but is no good over long distances.

The invention of the telephone had to wait until the telegraph system was well established. Researchers could then tackle the problems of sending the complex patterns of the human voice down a wire, instead of staying with systems such as the Morse code. The man who succeeded was Scottish-born Alexander Graham Bell (1847-1922), though by only a few hours. At the same time another inventor, Elisha Gray, was racing towards publishing his ideas; Bell gets the credit because he got to the American Patent office a short time before Gray!

▲ Alexander Graham Bell was born in Scotland, emigrating to the United States in 1870. Apart from his pioneering scientific work, he gave music lessons and taught deaf people how to speak.

▶ A replica of Bell's first telephone transmitter. Bell was helped with advice from Joseph Henry, and assisted by Thomas Watson. Bell and Watson were testing a new telegraph transmitter designed to send several messages at the same time – the first words were sent accidentally when Watson heard Bell shout that he had spilt acid down his clothes!

**B**ell's first telephone was based on the electromagnet, two of which were joined by wires. To use the machine, you spoke into a funnel-shaped chamber, in which the vibrations from your voice shook a thin, flat sheet of iron called a diaphragm. These small movements caused changes in the magnetic field of an electromagnet. The varying forces were then sent as an electrical signal to the receiver. This early system was soon replaced by the carbon microphone (shown in the diagram) which was much more efficient, and was largely responsible for the telephone's success.

Bell worked hard at letting people know about the telephone, both in America where he had perfected it, and in Britain and Europe, too. American response was dramatic, but the Europeans were not quite so keen. The existing telegraph system was regarded by many as being quite sufficient, especially as the sound quality of the early telephones was not good. Telephones were expensive to introduce, as each one needed its own connection, the wires had to be of better quality than telegraph lines, and telephone poles were prone to storm damage.

Even so, it was only a matter of time before the telephone caught on. In 1880 there were barely 33,000 telephones in the world, but ten years later there were over 400,000. Today, there are so many that the exact figure is not known, but it is probably around the 1,000 million mark.

## ☀ TELEPHONE EXCHANGES

The first telephones were connected to each other in pairs, with no way of linking to others. This was a very limited system, so the first telephone exchanges were built to improve things. Local lines went into an exchange office, where operators rerouted calls by switching sockets on a big board. To make an long-distance call, you always had to go through the operator.

As telephones grew in number, it became necessary to have lists of subscribers, and the first telephone directory was printed in Connecticut, USA, in 1878. Today, the most advanced directories, such as the French Minitel system, are entirely computer-based.

# RECORDING SOUND

The world's first recorded words were made by American inventor Thomas Alva Edison (1847-1931), saying the words, 'Mary had a little lamb'. With this poetic line, Edison made listening to recorded sound as easy as printing had made reading a book. Edison's list of inventions is still a record-breaker for one man – he took out no less than 1,097 patents. Most of them were improvements of existing machines, but sound recording was his own, unique contribution to improving the world's communications.

Edison called his machine the phonograph. It was an early version of the record player. Instead of flat discs, the phonograph used small cylinders, covered in a thin coat of wax. A sensitive needle recorded sound vibrations as a wriggling groove in the rotating cylinder. To play the recording, the needle tracked the same groove, replaying the sounds through a pair of headphones, or later, through a trumpet shaped horn. No electricity was needed for the first phonographs because the cylinder turned by clockwork.

▲ Thomas Edison started off his inventing career early – by the age of ten, he had a fully-equipped basement chemistry laboratory. His inventions included telegraphic printers, the phonograph and improvements to the telephone. Edison's phonograph used wax cylinders for record and replay.

1

2

◄▲ The vinyl record (1) stores vibrations directly in a spiral groove running round the disc. A needle tracks the groove, converting changes in the groove to sound patterns. A magnetic tape (2) changes patterns recorded in the tape to a form that matches the sound waves of the original.

After Edison's phonograph, sound recording, using discs and tapes, become a big industry. The magnetic tape recorder was invented in 1898 by Valdemar Poulsen from Denmark, who demonstrated his 'Telegraphone' at the 1900 Paris Exhibition, a huge show held to celebrate the dawn of the twentieth century. The machine recorded sounds as magnetised patterns on a moving steel tape. The Telegraphone was the forerunner of today's familiar tape recorder, but the idea had to wait for the electronic amplifier to be developed before it became practicable. Poulsen's machine was also the very first telephone answering machine – it was originally devised as a message-taker for the telephone, a device that was then less than 25 years old. As well as using tape, Poulsen was also the first to use a thin coating of powder that could be magnetised.

The tape recorder took a long time to become really popular, however – it was not until the 1950s, when cheap and tough plastic-based tapes became widely available, that home tape recording took off. With the 1960s-era compact cassette, pre-recorded music tapes sealed the beginning of the end for the vinyl record.

▲ In a modern recording studio, sound engineers have total control over the finished product. Sounds from voice and instruments can be adjusted, mixed and remixed, until exactly the right effect is achieved.

▲ Before power amplifiers were invented, record players used horn loudspeakers. The horn increased sound picked up by the needle like a megaphone.

# ☀ RADIO

In 1887, German scientist Heinrich Hertz showed that radio waves – invisible waves similar to light waves – existed. His experimental equipment proved that a spark of electricity also sent out a radio wave, like the ripples in a pond when you throw in a stone. What's more he discovered that the waves could be bent and reflected like light, even though you couldn't see them. And, most importantly, radio waves were fast – they travelled at the speed of light, about 300,000 km per second.

But though Hertz and other scientists carried out many experiments, there seemed to be no practical use for it. It was an Italian engineer, Guglielmo Marconi (1874-1937), from Bologna in Italy, whose discoveries led to the radios we use today. He started experimenting in his Bologna house in 1894, and soon succeeded in sending and receiving radio-wave transmissions over a distance of about 2.4 km. He tried to get the Italian government interested but was turned down, and in 1896 went to Britain where the potential of the equipment impressed William Preece, the post office chief engineer.

## ☀ BEATING THE STORMS

When Marconi and his team were preparing equipment for the first transatlantic radio message, they ran into trouble with bad weather. Storms broke the fragile aerials, and in Newfoundland, high-flying kites were used instead. To travel such a distance, the signals bounced off layers in the upper atmosphere.

▼ Marconi, photographed with his equipment.

The British government was slow in making up its mind about providing backing however, and Marconi went on to form his own company, the Wireless Telegraph and Signal Company to get things going. Progress was rapid as Marconi improved his equipment, and in 1901 he managed to send a signal from Cornwall in Britain to Newfoundland, Canada, a distance of 3,440 km. Marconi called his device the wireless telegraph, as no wires were used between the sender and receiver; Morse code was used to send messages.

▶ **You listened to an early radio receiver using a pair of headphones. Electronic amplifiers, with their ability to power big loudspeakers, were not generally available until the 1930s.**

A sensational murder case sealed the success of radio communication. In 1910, the ocean liner *Montrose* sailed across the Atlantic with murderer Dr Crippen as one of the passengers, fleeing from justice in Britain to a new life in Canada. Unknown to Crippen, the British police contacted the ship's captain by wireless, before boarding a faster ship to overtake the *Montrose*. Crippen's day-to-day shipboard life was splashed in newspapers on both sides of the Atlantic, without him knowing a thing about it. And no one was more surprised than Crippen when police eventually boarded the *Montrose* to arrest him!

▲ **Radio waves (1) are just a part of the electromagnetic spectrum, which also includes infra-red (2), which we feel as heat, and visible light (3) which our eyes detect.**

Two years later, another liner, the *Titanic*, sank on its maiden voyage after hitting an iceberg in mid-Atlantic. Hundreds of lives were lost, partly because the radio operator aboard the nearest ship was off-duty and did not hear the distress signals from the doomed ship. After the disaster, all ships were required to have a wireless and an operator on duty constantly, in case of emergency calls.

# BROADCASTING BEGINS

In 1906 many wireless operators were surprised to hear music instead of Morse code coming out of their headphones. This radio broadcast, by American physicist Reginald Fessenden, was the first time that anyone had heard anything but crackles and Morse code at long range. Fessenden's equipment had a range of some 300 km, but despite this it was years before public broadcasting started. Receiving equipment was not yet reliable enough for mass production, and no one had thought of using radio for interest and entertainment.

But the radio industry was booming as a commercial and emergency system. There were also many amateur radio enthusiasts (known as radio 'hams') and when some European hams started broadcasting entertainment instead of the usual serious fare, people (especially the makers of radio equipment) realised that there might be a big future in such transmissions.

▲ Long-distance broadcasting was made possible, as some types of radio wave bounce off layers in the upper atmosphere. Reception could be a hit and miss affair though, as such communications are easily affected by bad weather.

▶ Radio was a boom industry from the 1920s on. This 1949 radiogram (taken from an advertisement in a magazine of the time) was a popular gadget that combined radio receiver and record player. The nearest thing today is a ghettoblaster, which typically has radio, tape and compact disc functions.

◄ **Inside a transistor radio. An aerial picks up the signal. The electronic components are assembled on a circuit board. The loudspeaker is fixed to the plastic case.**

The British Broadcasting Corporation (BBC) was one of the pioneers of radio, sending out a mixture of news, theatre and music in the early 1920s. American and European stations filled the air waves too – in fact, the very first radio station was KDKA of Pittsburgh, USA, which started transmissions in 1921, a year before the BBC. By 1930, radio broadcasting was big business. Today there are thousands of stations, covering everything from rock and classical music to sports and current affairs.

Radio receivers have come a long way since the primitive equipment you could buy in the 1920s. The invention of the transistor in 1947 by a three-man American team allowed the production of radios that were small and reliable. Before the transistor, radios were mostly big and bulky devices that used fragile and unreliable valves in their circuits. Transistors marked the dawn of the electronic age, being cheap to make, very tough and reliable. They are used as switches or to amplify an electric current or voltage.

## ☀ TRANSISTOR PIONEERS

The transistor, with its triple advantages of small size, low cost and reliability fuelled the development of the electronic devices we use today. The transistor was developed by William Shockley (1910-1989), with John Bardeen and Walter Brattain. These scientists shared the 1956 Nobel Prize in Physics for their pioneering work in the field.

# ☀ RADAR AND SONAR

The idea for radar dates back to 1904, when German physicist Christian Helsmeyer suggested using reflected radio waves as an early warning system to prevent ships colliding at sea. Interesting as the idea was, there were no developments until the 1930s, when it was revived as a form of early warning system to detect enemy planes before they got within bombing range. In World War II, radar became a vital weapon in the armories of the fighting powers.

Radar, which stands for **ra**dio **d**etection **and r**anging, was first developed by a British team led by the Scottish scientist Robert Watson-Watt (1892-1973). By 1937, a chain of radar stations was being built along the south coast of Britain. The advantage of the system was that defending fighter planes could stay on the ground until needed, and could be directed to the enemy, without wasting time in a mid-air search.

▲ Ground-based radar is used to monitor aircraft near airports. The radar sends out a powerful pulse of radio energy (shown red in the diagram). Some of this is reflected back (shown blue) by the aircraft and received by the radar dish. The result is displayed as a glowing 'blip' on a radar screen.

▲ The AWACS (Airborne Warning And Command System) jets are among the most important of today's military aircraft. From a cruise height of 10 km, an AWACS can pinpoint hundreds of enemy air and land positions.

The first radar equipment was big and bulky, but before long, radar sets were made small enough to be carried aboard aircraft. Here they were used to detect enemy ships, submarines and other aircraft, especially at night. Today, virtually all aircraft bigger than light planes carry radar as standard. Weather radar allows the crew of an airliner to steer clear of particularly bad weather. Ground-based radar is used by air traffic controllers to steer planes safely to and from airports. Ships too, carry radar to steer clear of rocks and other obstructions.

▲ Sonar is an essential piece of equipment for many vessels, from fishing boats to nuclear submarines. This picture shows a computer-generated three-dimensional sonar display, which includes (believe it or not) an image of a fish on the left.

▲ The orange box is a towed sonar, about to be released from a research ship. It has a range of 2-3 km under water, and can even penetrate 70 metres through ocean-bottom sediment.

Sonar (from the words **so**und **n**avigation **a**nd **r**anging) is also a system that works by detecting reflections from objects. In this case, the reflections are echoes from short bursts of high-pitched sound, sent out by a transmitter. It was the sinking of the liner *Titanic* in 1912 that inspired scientists to find a way of detecting icebergs before they could do any damage. Submarine warfare during World War I made such an underwater warning system even more vital. French scientist Paul Langevin began experiments in Paris in 1915, and by 1916 had succeeded in producing ultrasonic (higher than human ears can detect) sound waves that could penetrate up to three kilometres under water. With careful tuning, Langevin found that his sonar equipment could detect shoals of fish and other underwater objects. It could also be used to measure the depth of the sea bottom under a ship, reducing the risk of running aground in shallow waters.

Sonar systems of today display returning echoes on a TV screen. There can be quite an art to understanding the meaning of the ghostly blue-grey image however – even a trained operator sometimes cannot tell the difference between a submarine and a large whale! Sonar is slower than radar – in water, sound waves travel at little more than 6,000 km/h. But despite this, sonar is of more use than even the most powerful radar, as few radio waves travel far under water.

# TELEVISION

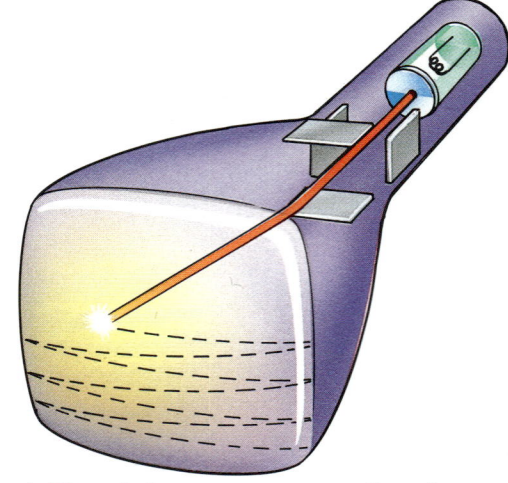

▲ The picture on a conventional TV screen is created by a glowing 'flying spot' that moves from side to side. As the spot zig-zags downwards, it creates an image. The process is repeated 25 times a second, so fast that we seem to see a steady picture. The spot appears when invisible particles called electrons hit the back of the screen. The screen is coated with a substance that glows briefly when struck by an electron.

**W**ith the success of radio, there remained a major communications target for researchers – transmitting moving pictures as well as sound. There was a precedent for the idea itself, as sending 'wire' pictures by telegraph had become common. Here, a picture was broken down into thousands of dots, which were transmitted one after another. It was a slow process however, and could not be used for television pictures.

In 1926 Scottish electronics pioneer John Logie Baird (1888-1946) came up with the first working television system. It used a spinning disc, combined with a photo-electric cell that changed the varying brightness of the image into electrical signals. The result was a rather fuzzy picture, which though much improved over the next few years, lost out to an electronic rival, the iconoscope.

▲ John Logie Baird, pictured with his experimental mechanical scanning television apparatus.

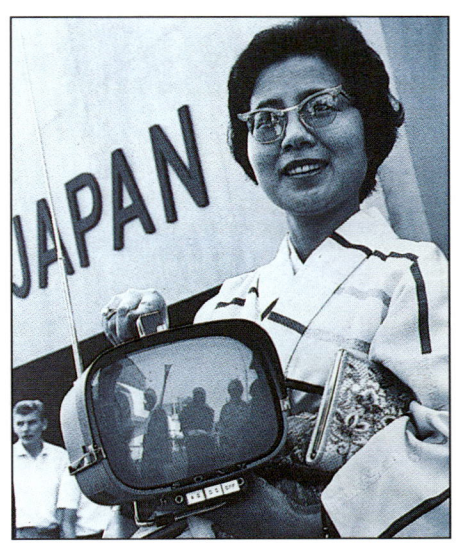

**V**ladimir Zworykin (1889-1982) was a Russian who moved to the USA in 1919. His iconoscope used electronic scanning to read an image, breaking it up into a number of 'lines', and displaying the result on a cathode-ray tube. This was a device that had been around since 1897, when it was invented by a German physicist, Karl Braun. A similar system became the basis of the first regular TV broadcasts, from London's Alexandra Palace, in 1937.

Broadcast television was almost entirely in black-and-white until 1953, when the American National Television Systems Committee (NTSC) adopted a workable colour system that split the picture into its primary colours of red, green and blue, using special mirrors. Electronic picture tubes put out three electric signals that varied with the brightness of these primary colours, and the three signals were combined to form a full-colour image by the receiving set.

Today several broadcasting systems compete with NTSC, including France's SECAM and PAL from Germany. The quality of the pictures are fairly similar (though PAL is generally reckoned the best), but if you have, say, a PAL TV set, then you cannot pick up NTSC broadcasts. Only special multi-standard receiving equipment can do this.

 **TELEVISION WORLD**

Television has allowed people to share some things in common. Commercially, TV advertising has enabled some manufacturers to make 'world brands' of their products. Satellite TV has made it easy to keep up to date with world news and pop music, provided that you have a satellite dish (see page 30). In China, however, the rulers have banned such dishes to much of the population, because they fear the unsettling effects of foreign TV programmes.

# VIDEO

**V**ideo is now the most popular way of recording sounds and pictures, especially programmes directly from television broadcasts, and movies for home replay. The first video recorder was developed in 1956 by a team working for the American Ampex corporation, a company that already made tape-recording equipment.

The video cassette recorder (VCR) stores images as well as sound on magnetic tape. It receives signals from an aerial and records pictures, 25 per second, as diagonal stripes across the tape. The sound is usually recorded at the edge of the tape, separate from the video signal. The first Ampex system used a bulky 50 mm-wide tape, but today home video cassette recorders mostly use the 12.65 mm-wide Home Video System (VHS) tape developed by the J Victor Company of Japan in the 1970s. There were several competitors for a universal home video system, including rivals from Philips in Holland and Sony in Japan, but the VHS system won the battle, largely because many other electronics manufacturers were allowed to build equipment under license. VHS literally swamped the competition.

▲ **Different types of video tape include high quality professional types (bottom), and home-use VHS and 8 mm (top).**

► **There are hundreds of different types of video recorder, but they all share similar parts. These include:**

**1 Video tape**
**2 Audio recording head**
**3 Video recording head**
**4 Guide rollers**
**5 Erase head**

Owning a VCR was fine, but what if you wanted to record your family and friends? The answer to that, up until the late 1970s, was a home-movie camera, which used narrow, 'bootlace' photographic film. Each reel was expensive, lasted just a few minutes and had to be developed by a specialist photographic shop. Also, the image was often fuzzy and wobbly, and film could break in the projector.

The answer to all this came in the form of the first wave of domestic video cameras – miniaturized VCRs that included lens and light-sensing electronics in a hand-held package. These came mostly from the big Japanese electronics companies, led by the Sony corporation in 1979. Various video camera ('camcorder') makers tried to outdo each other, but by the 1990s, just two recording formats ruled the camcorder market – VHS and the 8 mm system, from a team of companies headed by Sony. Both systems offer long recording times and the ability to erase and re-record unwanted material.

▶ The secret of a camcorder's ability to record light lies behind the lens. Here you can see the tiny CCD chip.

▲ A flat-screen TV monitor replaces the traditional viewfinder on this model, a Sharp ViewCam.

The camcorder's main technical advance is that it uses electronics to record the image. The CCD, or charge coupled device, uses an array of tiny light sensors, anything up to 800,000 on a chip just 17 mm across. As light from the lens falls on each one, a small electric current is set up, the varying current being translated into an electronic signal by complex circuits on the camcorder. The result is recorded onto tape, a frame at a time, in diagonal stripes, for later replay. This can be either in the camcorder or through a home video deck.

# TELECOMMUNICATIONS

Planet Earth is covered by an invisible spider's web of long-distance electronic links; they allow you to see TV programmes from far-off countries, and talk to someone half a world away with no more effort than it takes to speak to someone in the next room.

The story of long-distance communications began back in the nineteenth century, with the first telegraph systems. Intercontinental links started with the laying of the first transatlantic telegraph cable in 1858. People found the new links essential – by 1885 many more underwater cables had been laid and nearly two million telegrams were sent every week. Amazingly, the first telephone cable across the Atlantic was not laid until 1956; it provided just 36 interference-free telephone lines. A year later the space age began, with the launch of the Russian Sputnik I space satellite. With this, an idea first thought up in 1945 by the science-fiction writer Arthur C Clarke, began to take shape, that of using satellites high above the Earth as relay stations for radio messages.

▲ A microwave tower, often used for distances that do not require a satellite.

◀ An Earth station's dish sends out a radio beam to a satellite. For receiving a message, the same dish concentrates radio signals into the receiver electronics.

The new age of global communications dawned in 1962 with the launch of the first TV comsat, or communications satellite, the American Telstar 1. This ball-shaped comsat could relay signals aimed at it from a ground-based transmitter, around the curve of the world to an Earth station, waiting to receive the message. Telstar first relayed live TV signals across the Atlantic in 1962.

Telstar was followed a year later by Syncom 1, which did a similar job, but from a higher orbit. This was at a height of some 36,000 km, an altitude at which a satellite appears to stay in the same spot above the equator. Using just three comsats in this geostationary orbit – their positions form a huge triangle in space – a message can be sent anywhere on Earth in less than half a second. In fact, if you talk to someone on the other side of the world, the only clue to the distance involved is the very slight delay as you talk to each other. There are now dozens of comsats in geostationary orbit. They carry thousands of TV and telephone signals every moment of the day.

Back on Earth, microwave links can be used to relay signals over fairly short distances. Microwaves are radio waves that can be very tightly beamed, between towers that are in sight of each other, not unlike an electronic version of Chappe's optical telegraph.

◀ **Comsats have ranged in size from Telstar's metre width, to the Intelsat series, each of which is the size of a truck. Here an ASC comsat is launched from the cargo bay of the Space Shuttle _Discovery_. A long-distance telephone call goes from home to exchange, then to an Earth station, which beams the message into space. The satellite relays the signal across the world.**

# PHOTOCOPY AND FAX

**M**aking or sending a copy of a document used to be a fairly complicated affair. If you typed a story, you could use a sheet of coated carbon paper, sandwiched between your 'top copy' and the copy sheet. It was a dirty business, not helped by the fact that carbon paper was slippery stuff and often dropped between the sheets you were using. Sending a copy over a distance was even less convenient. You could send it by mail and be prepared to wait, or you could send a telegram. This involved either a trip to the telegraph office or arranging for collection by a messenger. The twin inventions of the photocopier and facsimile, or fax machine changed all that.

Most photocopiers use a process thought up in the 1930s by an American, Chester Carlson, who needed a copier that could reproduce not just words, but pictures too. Carlson was a lawyer who dealt with patent application forms, almost all of which included complex descriptions and diagrams of new gadgets and inventions. Carlson named his process xerography, after the Greek words *xeros*, meaning 'dry', and *graphos* meaning 'writing'.

▲ **Chester Carlson had some difficulties with his early experiments – he did not have enough money, the chemicals he used gave off dangerous fumes, and the neighbours complained! However, his hard work paid off, and on 22 October, 1938, he made the world's first successful xerographic copy, shown below. It shows the date and the New York area where he lived.**

▶ **The latest copiers work in colour and can also produce special effects, including these image distortions .**

Carlson's dry copier uses the principle of electrostatic attraction to do its job. This is similar to the way in which you can make a balloon pick up bits of paper if you rub it firmly. Inside the copier a metal plate is given a static charge and only conducts electricity when light shines on it. An image of the document to be copied is focused on the plate, until it carries an 'electric copy'. Black powder, called toner, is then sprayed at the plate, sticks to the charged parts, falls off the rest. Finally the toner is transferred to a sheet of paper pressed against it. A heater finishes off the job by baking the toner.

◄ This blow-up shows how a fax machine breaks down a photograph into tiny dots. The fax is widely used – some estimates reckon that nearly three-quarters of telephone calls between countries in the Pacific Ocean area are fax messages, not voice conversations. There are currently about three million fax machines world-wide.

The electronic fax (short for facsimile, or copy) machine uses telephone wires to send messages to other fax machines, anywhere in the world. A bright light scans the image, whether words, pictures or both but rather than create an exact copy, the fax breaks down the image into rows and rows of tiny dots. These are sent as fax code – like a faster, electronic version of Morse code – down the telephone line to a fax machine at the receiving end. Here, the dot code is received and printed out in lines of dots.

Most people, especially those in business, regard the fax as a great help, but for all the electronics, it is little more than a high-speed 'post-it' note. Its history helps explain this: as little as ten years ago, most Japanese business was conducted face-to-face, with documents written by hand rather than typed. Japanese alphabets contain thousands of picture symbols, and a 1970s 'typewriter' looked more like a full-scale typesetting machine than a desktop device. For this way of working, the fax was a natural as it allowed the written language to enter the age of high-speed communications.

# THE DIGITAL AGE

▲ A drawing of a Babbage calculating machine. This was never completed, as Babbage ran out of money to continue work on the project.

The computer is developing into probably the ultimate communications tool. A laptop word-processing computer was used to write this book, a desktop computer was used to design its pages. Still others were used at various print and production stages. We use computers in every part of our lives, yet all this has come about in little more than the last forty years, so how did it all happen?

The roots of computing really belong in the time involved in adding up long lists of figures. For over 300 years, various inventors tried to make the job quicker and less prone to error, by mechanizing it. The first known attempt at building a 'mathematics engine' was in 1642, when French mathematician and physicist Blaise Pascal (1623-1662) built a mechanical calculating machine. In 1805 Joseph Jacquard built an automatic loom that was used to control knitting machinery. In 1834, Charles Babbage (1792-1871) designed the first machine we might recognize as a computer.

◀ The most powerful early computers were huge. Today, an average laptop computer packs more punch than this room-sized machine of the 1950s.

**B**abbage was Professor of Mathematics at Cambridge University, Britain, and was so fired with enthusiasm for his invention that he resigned his post to work on the 'Difference Engine' full-time. In 1833, there was no such thing as an electronics industry, so Babbage's machine depended on sets of finely-made brass gears to produce answers to problems. Babbage thought up a second machine, the 'Analytical Engine', which was intended to solve algebra problems as well as simple sums. He worked on this for more than a decade, but it was never finished.

There are various competitors for the title of first modern computer. The first that used a stored program for operation was the Z3 of German Konrad Zuse, in 1941. The machine was used for military aircraft design. Two years later, the first electronic computer, called Colossus, was in use by the British, to help crack secret enemy codes. Colossus needed a team of engineers to keep things in working order, one of the jobs being to replace valves, which burnt out from time to time. Colossus had 1,500 of them, their job to act as switches and amplifiers in the circuits of the machine. In 1946, an American team built the 18,000-valve ENIAC, the first digital computer. This used binary code, the counting method that became the standard system.

 **COMPUTING PIONEER**

Charles Babbage was a man born ahead of his time – the technology that was available in the nineteenth century was not advanced enough for the demands of computer processing. But the idea behind his Analytical Engine, a machine that could be programmed with a set of instructions, that could process the mathematics involved, and that could output the result on paper, remains at the core of modern computing.

# SPEED AND POWER

The story of computing since the days of the 30-tonne ENIAC has been one of shrinking size combined with increasing power and speed – and it is all because of the electronic revolution started in 1948, by the team headed by American scientist Walter Brattein.

Before then, electronic devices (such as the radio) depended on delicate glass-and-metal valves to control and amplify the flow of electricity in their circuits. Brattein's brainchild was the transistor, a device that, because it was smaller, tougher and used less power, started to replace the valve. Once production got underway, transistors became far cheaper, too. Among the first wave of popular transistorized devices were the pocket-size radios of the early 1960s – you could now listen to your favourite music station or the latest news from a radio no bigger than the palm of your hand.

The next step towards today's computers was the integrated circuit. Even though transistors were small, they were still wired together in the old-fashioned way.

▶ Making an IC chip requires surgically-clean conditions. The slightest particle falling onto a microcircuit renders it useless.

The integrated circuit or IC puts transistors, together with other components and their connections, on a single wafer of silicon material, the famous 'silicon chip'. American electronics engineer Jack Kilby made the first integrated circuit in 1958, though an attempt at one using valve technology had been made by a German firm back in 1926. However, Kilby's components still had to be joined by hand. In 1959, a team headed by Robert Noyce discovered how to make an IC chip using the newly-developed planar process. This uses photographic techniques to create the tiny circuit patterns that go on to each chip.

Noyce's team managed to put just one transistor on its first silicon chip – a typical IC chip of today packs thousands of components on to a piece of material just a few millimetres square. Compared with a valve, only a tiny amount of heat is generated; even so, a desktop computer generally needs a fan to keep things cool. Microchip technology has led to a host of cheap and reliable communications devices including portable telephones, miniaturized televisions, CD players and many others.

◄ **A microscope-view of a silicon chip, the heart of a computer. Nearly half a million components are squeezed on to a space half the size of your thumb nail.**

# CD-ROM AND MULTIMEDIA

**H**igh-power and low-cost computing has led towards another communications revolution, multimedia, in which words, sounds, pictures and movies are combined in one electronic document. Using a multimedia encyclopedia, you can read about something, hear the noise it makes and see a short section of video. This makes multimedia a powerful learning tool, a giant leap from the printed word. Not that publications like books and magazines are likely to disappear – multimedia is an additional communications tool, rather than a direct replacement.

► Inside a CD player. The laser beam (shown in red) reads the spiral of pits buried in the underside of the compact disc.

**A**s computers get more powerful, so the programs for them get more complex, and the demand for storage capacity gets bigger, too. Until the early 1990s, 'floppy discs' containing information in magnetic form were enough for most purposes. But programs now need a new storage medium, the CD-ROM, a mouthful that stands for **c**ompact **d**isc, **r**ead-**o**nly **m**emory, meaning that a computer can read the information on the disc but does not record onto it. A program is stored as a coded spiral of tiny pits, buried in the plastic material of the disc. On a typical 120 mm-wide disc there are millions of pits – if you unwound the spiral, it would stretch nearly 5 km! A low-power laser beam reads the digital code into the computer. Each CD-ROM can store hundreds of times as much information as a conventional floppy disc.

▲ This ultra-close view of a compact disc shows the pits that are embedded inside the 2 mm-thick plastic.

The CD-ROM is based on the audio compact disc, invented by engineers at the Dutch Philips company in the late 1970s. In 1980, Philips joined up with Sony of Japan, and the two companies brought out the first CDs soon after, aimed at the well-heeled hi-fi enthusiast. The CD has now almost entirely replaced the pressed-vinyl disc, used on the old record players.

CD-ROMs may be the best way of presenting information on screen, but if you want to search for information yourself, then one of the best tools could be the Internet. This is a network of tens of thousands of computers, spanning the globe. It is used by individuals, universities, commercial organizations and government departments. People using the Internet number 25 million or more, a figure that is rising all the time.

On the Internet you can find details of any subject you care to name. In fact, the ocean of information is so vast that the biggest difficulty can be finding things – you often need a special tracker program to hunt down a particular information source. As well as using the Internet as a vast library, people also talk to each other on it, a sort of electronic pen-pal system. Various codes and signals are used by Internet users, including 'smileys' such as this one – :-). Look sideways to see if the author is happy or not!

# NEW FRONTIERS

Computers have already linked the world together in a global information network, and it is likely that more people and computers will become joined like this in the future. This electronic sea of information is called cyberspace, a term coined by Canadian science-fiction writer William Gibson in the 1980s. Gibson foresees a future in which we will be able to submerge in this 'parallel universe', using computer-imaging machinery, to make it look and feel as real as the everyday world around us.

Virtual reality – VR – is a technology that provides the essential link with the electronic world of cyberspace. Wearing a pair of VR goggles for vision, and a VR glove for touch, you can already enter a computer program as if it were real life. The most popular use for VR so far is for gaming, where you can, for example, 'fly' a fast jet without ever leaving the ground.

▲ LunaCorps moon buggy, designed for do-it-yourself drivers on the Moon.

One commercial company is following up the VR idea with an interactive space exploration plan. LunaCorps aims to launch a moon buggy by Russian rocket in 1997, landing it at the site where Neil Armstrong first stepped on the Moon, in 1969. Some science experiments are planned for the buggy, but for most of the time, people will pay to drive it around the Moon using video links and VR goggles.

Virtual Research

▲ **VR goggles help this biochemist visualize a complex molecular structure.**

Computers which recognize speech and handwriting are already in use, though they need to improve dramatically before the finger-operated keyboard becomes extinct. And now there is a worldwide race to produce thought-controlled computers. The American Brainlink system is one of the first fruits of this race. The brain's tiny electrical impulses are picked up by sensors attached to the head, and are then relayed to the Brainlink computer.

Among the things that Brainlink can do is to help athletes improve their performance. Apparently, people can be trained to produce types of brain patterns that improve their chances of winning. It is a short step from this to being able to use Brainlink for steering a vehicle, and the advantages for disabled people could be enormous. At present the machine uses wire connectors, but soon long-range radio equipment may allow thought-control at a distance.

## ☀ MICRO-SIZE HELPERS

Personal digital assistants, or PDAs, will become popular in the near future. As yet, PDAs (the Apple Newton was one of the first), are limited in what they can do, but future models will recognize speech and writing, and communicate with other computers anywhere on Earth, via satellite links.

# TIMELINE OF ADVANCE

Here are some of the people, discoveries, inventions and improvements have brought about the world of today.

**Ancient Egypt** (about 3000 BC) Hieroglyphic picture writing and papyrus writing material developed. The first hieroglyphics date back to about 3000 BC; the latest example was from about AD 394. An even earlier form of picture writing was the cuneiform script used by the Sumerians in about 4000 BC.

**Ancient China** (about 105 AD) First use of paper making. Early forms of printing developed.

**Johannes Gutenberg** German printer (about 1400-1468). Invented the European printing press with movable type, after experiments in the 1440s. His most famous work was the Mazarin Bible, which he produced with Johann Fust.

**William Caxton** English printer (about 1422-1491). Learned about printing from Gutenberg and set up the first printing press in England in 1476. Printed about 100 different titles, including works by Geoffrey Chaucer and translations of the Roman statesman Cicero.

**Blaise Pascal** French mathematician and physicist (1623-1662). Made the world's first mechanical calculator in 1643. Also studied the effects of pressure, and invented the hydraulic press.

**Robert Hooke** British scientist (1635-1703). Investigated among other things, the elasticity of materials (such as springs), and invented the universal joint. Suggested a type of telephone involving two cans, joined by a length of string or wire.

**Claude Chappe** French engineer (1763-1805). Devised an optical telegraph for the French military. It was the first system to be called a telegraph, from the Greek words *tele*, meaning 'far' and *graphein* 'to write'. Other telegraph pioneers include Baron Schilling, who devised an electric telegraph and built a line in Russia in the 1830s.

**Jean-François Champollion** French scholar (1790-1832).

Cracked the secrets of the three forms of early writing inscribed in the ancient Egyptian Rosetta stone. His approach to translation work was criticised for many years, and it was not until the 1860s that other archaeologists admitted that his techniques worked.

**Samuel Morse** American inventor (1791-1872). Devised the dot-dash code system for the electric telegraph, first demonstrating it in 1837. It has since become the international standard.

**Charles Babbage** Mathematics professor (1792-1871). A pioneer of computing who designed a pair of machines intended to speed up mathematical calculations. Highly regarded as a computing pioneer.

**Joseph Henry** American teacher and physicist (1797-1878). A pioneer of electricity research, he invented a type of electric telegraph and the first practical electric motor. He became the first director of the famous Smithsonian Institution, in Washington, USA.

**Charles Wheatstone** British scientist (1802-1875). Invented a practical electric telegraph with William Cooke, in 1837. He also devised a viewer for three-dimensional pictures.

**Louis Braille** French teacher (1809-1852). Devised the raised-dot system by which blind people can read books, in 1829. Braille himself was blind. The earliest raised-letter printing was thought up by Valentine Haüy (1745-1822).

**Julius Reuter** German news gatherer (1816-1899). First worked as a bank clerk, and in 1849, began sending stock exchange prices in Europe, first by carrier pigeon, then by electric telegraph. Opened a news agency office in London, in 1851.

**Alexander Graham Bell** Scottish-American teacher and inventor (1847-1922). Invented the first telephone in 1876, which worked by changing sound into electrical signals, and back again into sound. Thomas Edison soon produced a better design, which was much more successful.

**Thomas Alva Edison** American inventor (1847-1931). A prolific inventor who took out almost 1,300 patents. Invented the first phonograph in 1877, using money from another invention of his, a telegraphic printer.

**Heinrich Hertz** German scientist (1857-1894). First person to broadcast and receive radio waves, in 1887, using specially-developed electric-spark equipment.

**Guglielmo Marconi** Italian scientist (1874-1937). Invented the wireless telegraph, a system that could send messages over long distances without wires. In 1901, his radio equipment transmitted Morse code signals across the Atlantic Ocean, from Cornwall, England, to Newfoundland, Canada.

**John Logie Baird** Scottish engineer (1888-1946). In 1924, he became the first person to transmit a television picture using radio waves, and in 1928, was the first to send a picture across the Atlantic. Despite these early successes, Baird's mechanical TV scanner was beaten commercially by the system developed by Vladimir Zworykin.

**Vladimir Zworykin** Russian-American physicist and electronic engineer (1889-1982). Helped develop the television camera and picture tube. The electronic TV system was a big improvement over Baird's scanner. Zworykin also developed the electron microscope, a vastly more powerful machine than the traditional type.

**Robert Watson-Watt** British engineer (1892-1973). The man who developed radar, filing a patent for radio direction-finding in 1919. In 1935 he headed a team to 'develop a system for locating aircraft in all weathers and by day or night by radio waves', what was later to be generally known as radar. His work was of great value in World War II. After that war, Watson-Watt developed radar for peaceful roles.

**Chester Carlson** American lawyer (1906-1968). Devised the xerographic system of dry-copying. His first copy was made in 1938, but the first commercial copiers using his system were not produced until the 1950s. It is now the most widely-used copy system of all.

**William Shockley** English-American physicist (1910-1989). Together with fellow scientists John Bardeen and Walter Brattain, invented the transistor in 1947, opening the way for the electronic world of today.

**Arthur C. Clarke** Science fact and fiction writer (1917-). First thought up the idea of using satellites for long-distance communications, in 1945. Since then, has written many books on futuristic themes and has had movies made of several of his books, including the classic 2001 A Space Odyssey, filmed by director Stanley Kubrick. Other influential writers include the Canadian William Gibson, whose 'cyberpunk' style previews the computerized world of the near future.

◄ **Vladimir Zworykin**

A ready-reference guide to many of the terms used in this book.

**Archaeology** Scientific study of the life of ancient peoples, carried out principally by excavating the sites of cities and dwellings.

**Binary code** Counting system used by computers, consisting of 'strings' of code that use combinations of just two numbers or digits, 0 and 1. Any device (such as a computer) that uses this system is therefore known as a digital machine.

**Braille** System of raised letter code, to make reading possible for blind people. It was invented by Louis Braille in the nineteenth century.

**Carbon microphone** Type of microphone commonly used in telephones.

**Cathode-ray tube** The familiar TV display system, as used in the home and for computer and radar screens. Streams of electrons from the rear of the tube hit the inside of the front, where a special coating causes the screen to glow. Often abbreviated as CRT. The latest picture tube system uses thousands of miniaturized CRTs to provide the picture, instead of just one. The result? A tube just 10 cm thick.

**CCD** Charged couple device, as used in camcorders. The CCD uses an array of up to 800,000 tiny light sensors, all mounted on an individual 'imaging chip', usually about 17 mm across. The sensors convert the light falling on them to an electric current, larger or smaller, depending on the intensity of light. This is fed into the camcorder's complex circuits, eventually to be recorded on video tape.

**CD-ROM** Compact disc-read only memory. The latest type of compact disc, especially suited to store computer information for multimedia presentations. Stores the digital information as a spiral of microscopically-small pits in the disc.

**Comsat** Communications satellite, designed as a relay station in space for radio and TV signals. The first artificial satellite, the Russian Sputnik I, was launched in 1957; there are now hundreds of satellites in orbit, their functions ranging from communications duties to 'sky spy' photographic missions for military purposes.

▲ The increasing amount of information being passed around the world is overloading conventional telephone lines. To cope with demand, 'information superhighways' of a material called optical fibre are being laid. This can carry over 30,000 times more information than a telephone wire of the same width. Find out more on this subject in Science Discovery *Optics*.

**Cyberspace** Term for the 'ocean' of computerized information that is now available for users. The word comes from cybernetics (from the Greek *kybernetes*, meaning 'helmsman'), which compares complex computer systems with the human nervous system.

**Earth station** The ground link between the user and a comsat. Earth stations can be spotted by their dish-shaped aerials.

**Electric telegraph** Long distance communications system that uses electricity passing down a wire. Various types were developed, mostly in the nineteenth century.

**Electromagnet** A magnet consisting of a soft iron core around which a coil of insulated wire is wound. If a current is passed down the wire the core is magnetized.

**Electronics** The study of devices that depend on the controlled flow of electrons (tiny parts of atoms) to make them work.

**Electrostatics** The study of electric charges that are at rest and the forces that act between them. Examples of electrostatic attraction include the rubber balloon, which will attract small pieces of fluff and paper when you rub it.

**Geostationary orbit** An orbit used by many comsats, some 36,000 km above the Earth's equator, where the speed of a satellite matches the speed of the earth's rotation. The

◄ Situated 36,000 km above the equator, geostationary orbit allows a trio of comsats to cover all the globe except the poles.

result is that the satellite remains in one spot above the earth.

**Heaviside layer** A part of the earth's atmosphere 50-90 km up, that reflects some radio waves, allowing signals to go beyond the horizon.

**Hieroglyphics** A method of writing that used pictures and symbols to represent words and sounds. Used especially in ancient Egypt.

**Iconoscope** The electronic picture tube invented by Vladimir Zworykin. It competed with John Logie Baird's mechanical scanner system in the early days of television.

**Integrated circuit** A miniature electronic circuit, widely used in

electronic equipment such as computers and calculators. Integrated circuits are often referred to simply as IC 'chips'.

**Internet** Global network of linked computers. Used as a library, notice board and general communications tool by computer users.

**Laser** Beam of intense light. Unlike ordinary light, laser light is 'coherent' – the light is one pure colour and the rays move in parallel. This means that a laser beam remains as a tight beam, and does not spread out like, for example, a torch beam. Lasers do not have to be powerful to be useful, however – a compact disc player uses a very low-power laser to read information on the disc.

**Modem** A machine that converts computer data into a form that can be transmitted down a telephone line. It can also be used to receive information.

**Mongols of Asia** A powerful empire, based in the heart of eastern Asia, that grew to great power in the thirteenth century under the command of Genghis Khan. The Mongols used a horse relay system to carry urgent communications, an idea copied by the US Pony Express of the nineteenth century.

**Morse code** Dot-dash alphabet first devised by Samuel Morse in 1837. It was very useful for the electric telegraph, but is also used for communications by radio, flag, and lamp.

**Multimedia** Electronic document, usually delivered on CD-ROM, that presents information in words, pictures, movies and sounds.

**Nobel Prize** Group of five annual awards, given for the best work in physics, chemistry, medicine, literature and the cause of universal peace. Named after Alfred Nobel, a Swedish inventor and chemist who had made a fortune from explosives and oil, the prizes were first awarded in 1901.

**Papyrus** African plant that grows to a height of one to three metres. It was used by the ancient Egyptians, Greeks and Romans as writing material.

**Patent** A right to make and sell an invention without competition from others who might try to make copies of it. Patent applications are made through Patent Offices, who carefully check to make sure that applications are for new and original ideas. Patents must be obtained in every country where protection is required.

**PDA** Personal digital assistant, the name for hand-held computer 'organisers'. Typically, a PDA has a small screen, can plug into a modem and bigger computers and has some form of handwriting recognition ability – necessary because it has no keyboard.

**Printed circuit board** Piece of material on which all or most of an electronic device's circuits are wired together. Particularly useful, as PCBs can often be slotted in and out of a machine, making repairs quick and easy.

**Radio wave** One part of the electromagnetic spectrum, which includes radio, visible light and x-rays. Such electromagnetic waves travel at the speed of light, about 300,000 km/s.

**Solar cell** An electric device that produces electricity from the energy in light.

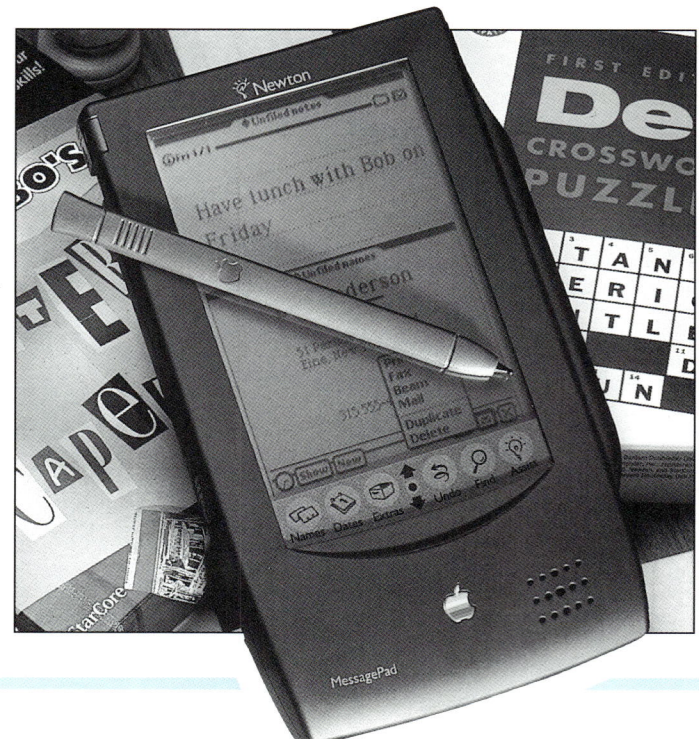

◀ **One of the first PDAs, the Apple Newton of 1993.**

**Telegraph** Device for sending messages long distances. It uses an electric current which passes along a wire linking a transmitter and receiver.

**Television format** Type of transmission system. There are three main TV formats in the world. NTSC is used in North America and Japan. PAL offers a crisper picture, and is used in much of the rest of the world. SECAM is used in France and some east European countries.

**Teleworker** Person who uses electronic telecommunications equipment to avoid the need to travel to an office every day.

**Transistor** Tiny device that can act as a switch or amplifier in an electric circuit. Transistors are basic components in electronic equipment.

**Vacuum tube** Electronic component, such as a valve or cathode ray tube, that has had the air extracted from its interior.

**Valve** Device for controlling the flow of electricity in an electrical circuit. Valves have now been almost universally replaced by transistors, which are smaller, cheaper and more reliable.

**Video format** The size, shape and electronic type of a particular recording system. The VHS format from the J. Victor Company of Japan is the type that is most widely used in home cassette recorders. TV companies use others, all of higher quality. For domestic camcorders, VHS and 8 mm are used, both also made in high-band versions, which offer improved picture quality.

▲ **Television programmes were first broadcast by the BBC in 1936, from London's Alexandra Palace transmitter, shown here.**

## ☀ GOING FURTHER

**Books** The subject of communications is not well covered in single comprehensive titles, and information tends to be scattered about in specialist publications. These books will help you get started:
*Science Encyclopedia*, Dorling Kindersley 1993
*Pocket Book of Science* by Robin Kerrod, Kingfisher 1990
**Magazines** General-interest science magazines usually have a feature or two on the latest communications technology. Try the following:
*Focus* Snippets of information on just about every subject under the sun. Monthly.
*Popular Science* Packed with good articles, great

pictures, glossy diagrams and charts. Monthly.
*New Scientist* A more serious approach, and highly regarded by scientists. Weekly.
**Places** In Britain, museums with a science bent include the famous *Science Museum* in London and the newer, 'hands-on' *Eureka* museum in Halifax. For satellite fans, the Earth station at Goonhilly Down, Cornwall, has a fascinating visitor centre.
**CD-ROM** The title list is growing, but there is little that is directly to do with communications. However the Grolier *Encyclopedia* has many interesting entries, as does the Microsoft *Encarta*. Both feature animations, video clips, text and pictures.

# INDEX